The Tragedy of Hamlet, Prince of Denmark

Illustrated by: Suman S. Roy
Compiled and Edited by: Tapasi De

Contents

1. Hamlet, at a Glance — 3

2. Who's Who in the Play — 5

3. Hamlet, Prince of Denmark — 8

4. Post-reading Activities — 38

5. About the Author — 40

Hamlet at a Glance

The Tragedy of Hamlet, Prince of Denmark, one of Shakespeare's most well-known tragedies has often been categorized as a *revenge tragedy* by critics as the basic theme is that of revenge. The play also conforms to other features like murder, madness, play-within-a-play and the like.

Drama basically can be divided into three genres—comedy, tragedy and satire. A tragedy is a play that is based on human suffering. It is a literary work in which the main character is destined to get ruined and

Glossary
Revenge the action of harming someone in return for an injury done by them

hence he suffers extreme sorrow.

Hamlet has all the elements of a proper tragedy with the theme of revenge. The intensity of its situations, the suffering of Hamlet, the treachery of his mother Gertrude and Hamlet's strong desire for revenge makes this play of Shakespeare a timeless classic.

Who's Who in the Play

Hamlet

Hamlet, the central character of the play is undoubtedly the greatest dramatic character ever created. Hamlet is full of faults. But all these seemingly negative qualities such as indecisiveness, hastiness, hatred, brutality, and obsession make Hamlet a memorable character.

Claudius

Hamlet's major enemy is Claudius his uncle who is a shrewd, lustful, clever King who contrasts sharply with the other male characters in the play.

Glossary
Indecisiveness inability to take decisions
Obsession to be haunted, preoccupied or filled with an idea or emotion
Shrewd having sharp powers of judgement, cunning

Gertrude

Gertrude, is the beautiful Queen of Denmark and the mother of Hamlet who hastily marries her brother-in-law (Hamlet's uncle) Claudius. She is a hypocrite and is disloyal.

Ophelia

Ophelia is the beautiful daughter of Polonius, the Chamberlain. Her love for Hamlet is true and pure but sadly, it is not returned by Hamlet.

Polonius

Polonius is the father of the beautiful lady Ophelia whom Hamlet loves. He is the elderly Lord Chamberlain and chief counsellor of Claudius.

Glossary
Chamberlain an officer who looked after the household of a monarch or a noble
Counsellor a person who gives guidance on personal or psychological problems

The Ghost

The ghost is none other than the old King Hamlet who has been murdered. He appears and tells Hamlet the entire story of his murder. A major supernatural element which takes the play forward.

Horatio

A common man, Horatio went to school with Hamlet and remains his loyal best friend.

Laertes

Laertes is Polonius' son and Ophelia's brother.

Glossary
Supernatural something which is not natural and cannot be explained

Hamlet, Prince of Denmark

The story of Hamlet is set in the castle of Elsinore in Denmark. It began when Hamlet's mother Gertrude, Queen of Denmark, became a widow by the sudden death of King Hamlet. In less than two months after his death, Queen Gertrude married his brother Claudius. The people of Denmark considered this action at that time to be strange and insensitive. This was more so for Claudius did

Glossary
Widow a woman who has lost her husband by death
Insensitive showing or feeling no concern for the emotions of others

not resemble her late husband in the qualities of his character or his mind. He was as contemptible in his outward appearance as he was base and unworthy in his disposition. Many people even started suspecting that Claudius had deliberately killed his brother in order to get married to his widow and also to ascend the throne of Denmark. He very tidily did this keeping aside young Hamlet, the son of the dead king and lawful successor to the throne.

The cruel action of the Queen getting married so soon affected the young Prince Hamlet very much as he dearly loved his father and he worshipped him almost to idolatry! And, so he took to heart this unworthy conduct of his mother Gertrude. He lost all his joys and all his good looks as he was immersed in grief for his father's death and shame for his mother's marriage. Hamlet lost all pleasure in reading books, his princely exercises and sports. He grew weary of the world, which seemed to him like an unweeded garden, where all the wholesome flowers were choked up and nothing but weeds could thrive. Hamlet was not saddened by the fact that being the lawful heir to his father's throne, he was kept aside by his uncle. But what

Glossary
Contemptible deserving contempt or hatred
Disposition any person's inborn qualities of mind and character
Successor a person or thing that comes before another

pained him was that his mother had completely wiped off his father's memory! She had completely forgotten such gentle a husband! During his lifetime she had always appeared as loving and obedient a wife to him. And now within two months, or less than two months, she had married his uncle, which was a highly improper and unlawful marriage as they were related closely. Moreover, the haste with which his mother had chosen her new husband appeared to be extremely indecent and Hamlet found it hard to bear.

Hamlet's mother Gertrude or the new King could do nothing to divert his attention. He appeared in court in a suit of deep black, as his mourning for his father's death, was not yet over for him unlike his mother. Even on the day of his mother's marriage, he did not join any of the festivities or rejoicings as it appeared to him to be a disgraceful day.

What troubled him most was an uncertainty about the manner of his father's death. It was told by Claudius that a snake had bitten him. But young Hamlet had shrewd suspicions that Claudius had murdered him for his crown! He also began doubting his mother whether the murder was done by her consent or not!

Glossary
Indecent not decent and morally offensive

Days passed in tremendous mental agony when one day Hamlet heard a rumour that an apparition, resembling his father, had been seen by the soldiers who were guarding, on the platform before the palace at midnight. This happened for two or three nights

Glossary
Apparition a strange ghost or ghostlike image appearing suddenly

successively. 'How can this be? My dear father is dead and gone forever!' thought Hamlet. The figure came constantly clad in the same suit of armour, from head to foot, which the dead king was known to have worn. And they who saw it (Hamlet's bosom friend Horatio was one) agreed to this fact. They all said that it came just as the clock struck twelve; that it looked pale, had a sorrowful face; that its beard was grisly and black, as they had seen it in his lifetime.

When they spoke to it; yet once they thought it lifted up its head and was about to speak. But that very moment the morning cock crew and it vanished out of their sight!

The young prince, though strangely amazed at all this, did not disbelieve. He concluded that it was his father's ghost which they had seen. He determined to take his watch with the soldiers that night, that he might have a chance of seeing it. He thought, 'If it is his father's ghost that they have seen, then I must say it has come with a purpose. It must be having something important to tell! Though now it is quiet, but it will speak surely.' And so, he waited restlessly for the night to come.

Glossary
Grisly terrifying

When night came, he stood with Horatio and Marcellus, one of the guards, upon the platform, where this apparition was accustomed to walk. The night was cold, and the air unusually biting. Hamlet and Horatio and their companion began talking about the coldness of the night, when suddenly Horatio said, 'There it comes!'

At the sight of his father's spirit Hamlet was struck with a sudden surprise and fear. He at first called upon the angels and heavenly ministers to defend them. But he gradually assumed more courage. And his father as it seemed to him, looked upon him so piteously, as if it wanted to talk to Hamlet. He looked exactly like himself as he was when he lived. Hamlet could not help addressing him.

He called him by his name, 'Hamlet, King, Father! Tell me father why did you have to leave your grave when you should have rested in peace? Let us know if there is anything which we can do to give peace to your spirit.'

Hearing this, the ghost called Hamlet, to take him to a place where they might be alone. Horatio and Marcellus tried to dissuade the young prince from following it, for they feared it to be some evil spirit who would throw

Glossary
Accustomed usual or habitual
Dissuade convince someone not to do something

him into the neighbouring sea or from the top of some dreadful cliff, and compel him to die. But their requests could not alter Hamlet's determination, who cared too little about his life. And so, like a courageous lion he followed the spirit to wherever it led him.

And finally, when they were alone together, the spirit broke silence! It said, 'I am your father King Hamlet and I have been cruelly murdered by your own Uncle Claudius. He always wanted to take my place. On the day of my murder, I was sleeping in the garden like any other day. Claudius poured the juice of poisonous henbane plant into my ears. This juice is so very poisonous that it travels through all the veins of the body poisoning it. Thus sleeping, I was cut off at once from my crown, my queen, and my life by my own brother!'

And he adjured Hamlet, 'If you have ever loved your dear father, you will revenge this foul murder!' The ghost also lamented to his son that his mother should so fall off from virtue so as to marry his murderer!

But he cautioned Hamlet, that by no means should he be violent against his mother, but to leave her to Heaven for justice. Hamlet promised to observe

Glossary
Cautioned to give a warning

the ghost's direction in all things and the ghost disappeared.

When Hamlet was left alone he took up a solemn resolution that nothing should remain in his brain

but the memory of what the ghost had told him and asked him to do. Hamlet related the particulars of this conversation to none other but his dear friend Horatio. He asked both him and Marcellus to keep this fact a secret that they had seen the ghost of the King.

The terror which the sight of the ghost had left upon the senses of Hamlet, misbalanced his mind completely. He being weak and dispirited already due to the sudden death of his father and his mother's marriage. And now he found it difficult to digest the shock of seeing his father's ghost. This made Hamlet very nervous thinking that his Uncle Claudius would start suspecting him that he was planning revenge against him or the fact that Hamlet knew all about his father's death!

Fearing all this, Hamlet took up a strange resolution that he would feign madness so that his uncle would never suspect him of plotting against him. From that time, Hamlet added quite an amount of wildness and strangeness in his dress, his speech and behaviour. He did this so excellently that the King and Queen were both deceived. But they did not think that father's sudden death was sufficient cause to produce such a

Glossary
Feign to pretend

behaviour. And so they concluded that it must be love. At last they were satisfied that they had found out the real reason of Hamlet's queer behaviour.

Before Hamlet fell into the sadness caused due to his father's death and his mother's second marriage, he loved a fair maiden called Ophelia. Ophelia was the daughter of Polonius, the King's chief counsellor in affairs of the state. He had sent her letters and rings, and made many tender show of his affection to her. Ophelia too believed in his love and vows.

But when Hamlet got drowned in grief, he neglected her. He deliberately treated her with unkindness and rudeness. But Ophelia being a very nice girl never reproached him but thought that it was a part of the disease of his mind.

One day Hamlet realised that he had been very unreasonably harsh in his treatment of this gentle lady. So he wrote her a letter full of wild starts of passion, showing his affection for this honored lady.

Ophelia dutifully showed this letter to her father and said, 'Father, look Prince Hamlet does love me!' And the old man thought it necessary to show it to the

Glossary
Reproached to blame somebody for something

King and the Queen, who from the very beginning supposed that the true cause of Hamlet's madness was love. When Queen Gertrude and Claudius heard this, they were pleased.

'I am quite certain that the beauty of Ophelia will restore him to his accustomed way,' said Queen Gertrude.

But Hamlet's malady lay deeper than she supposed. His father's ghost, which he had seen, still haunted his imagination. The thought to revenge, gave him no rest till it was accomplished. Every hour of delay seemed to him a sin and a violation of his father's commands. But planning the King's murder was no easy matter as he was always surrounded by guards or his Queen, Hamlet's mother. Besides, the very fact that the usurper was his mother's husband, filled him with grief and hatred. The mere thought of putting a fellow-creature to death was terrible to a gentle person like Hamlet. The intense grief from which he suffered produced strange doubts in his mind whether he should take revenge or not. Moreover, he could not help having some doubts in his mind, whether the spirit which he had seen was indeed his father's, or some devil's, who had the power to take any form as he pleased.

When Hamlet was in such a mental dilemma, a group of actors came to the royal court. Hamlet formerly used to take delight in their performances and particularly hearing one of them speak a tragical speech, describing the death of old Priam, King of Troy, with the grief of Hecuba, his queen. Hamlet

Glossary
Hatred strong dislike

welcomed his old friends, the actors, and remembering how that speech had formerly given him pleasure, requested the player to repeat it. They did repeat it in a very lively a manner, showing the cruel murder of the feeble old king, with the destruction of his people and city by fire. They also depicted the mad grief of the old queen, running barefoot up and down the palace, with a poor clout upon that head where a crown had been, and with nothing but a blanket upon her loins instead of her royal robes. This drew tears from all who stood by and watched, as it was played like the real scene. Even the actor himself delivered it with a broken voice and real tears.

Now seeing the performance of these actors, Hamlet began reflecting that if a player could work himself up to such deep feelings that too in a play, then he should also do something as he had a real motive! And while he thought about actors and acting, and the powerful effects which a good play has upon the spectator, he remembered an incident. In this incident, some murderer, who, seeing a murder on the stage, was so much affected by the resemblance of circumstances that he confessed his crime which he had committed!

Glossary
Destruction the action of destroying
Spectator a person who watches something—at a show, a game, or any other event
Resemblance the state of being alike
Confessed to admit that one has done something wrong

And so, Hamlet decided that these players should play something like the murder of his father before his uncle, and he would watch narrowly what effect it would have upon him. And from his looks Hamlet would be able to gather with more certainty if his uncle was the murderer or not. And so at once, he ordered a play to be prepared with the same story as his father's death and invited the King and Queen to watch it on a decided day.

The story of the play was based on the murder of a duke done in Vienna. The duke's name was Gonzago and his wife's, Baptista. The play showed how one Lucianus, a near relation of the duke, poisoned him in his garden for his estate, and how the murderer got the love of Gonzago's wife immediately after his death.

When the play was finally staged on the decided day, the King, who did not know the trap which was laid for him, was present with his Queen and the whole court. Hamlet sat near him to observe his reactions closely. The play began with a conversation between Gonzago and his wife. In this conversation, the lady made many promises of love, and of never marrying a second husband if she should outlive Gonzago.

She also wished that she should be cursed if she ever took a second husband. She also added that no woman would do so except those wicked women who kill their first husbands.

Just then, Hamlet observed the King his uncle to change colour at this expression. But when Lucianus, according to the story, came to poison Gonzago who was sleeping in the garden, the King became

restless. The strong resemblance which it bore to his own wicked act upon the late King, his brother, whom he had poisoned in his garden, struck him so severely that he was unable to sit for the rest of the play! He commanded for lights to his chamber, and he announced that he felt a sudden sickness. Abruptly, he left the theater. When the king had left, the play was considered over.

Now, Hamlet had seen enough to be satisfied that the words of the ghost were true and there was no illusion. And in a fit of happiness, like that which comes over a man who suddenly has some great doubt resolved, he swore to Horatio that he would take the ghost's word for a thousand pounds. But before he could even plan his revenge, Hamlet was called by the Queen his mother, to a private conference.

It was the King's desire that the queen should send for Hamlet, and tell him how much his late behaviour had displeased them both. And the King, wishing to know all that happened in that conference, and thinking that the Queen would not tell him, ordered Polonius, the old counsellor of state, to hide himself in the Queen's room. This command particularly pleased Polonius,

Glossary
Illusion something that creates a false impression of reality

who was a man grown old in crooked policies of state. He was delighted to get such an opportunity to get such a valuable information in such an indirect and cunning way.

When Hamlet came to his mother, she began to complain to him about his actions and behaviour. 'We are thoroughly offended by your behaviour lately, son! Do you know how much you have displeased your father?'

Hamlet, shocked that she should give such an honored name as 'father' to a wretch who was no better than the murderer of his true father, replied, 'Mother, YOU have much offended MY FATHER.'

'Son, have you forgotten whom you are speaking to?' asked the Queen, shocked.

'Alas!' replied Hamlet, 'I wish I could forget. You are the Queen, your husband's brother's wife; and you are my mother. I wish you were not what you are!'

'All right then,' said the Queen, 'if you show me so little respect, I will set those to you that can speak!' Saying this, she began to send for the King or Polonius.

Glossary
Information facts provided about something or someone

But Hamlet would not let her go, till he had tried to mend her wicked ways with his words. He held her by her hand and made her sit down. Now the Queen was very frightened by this manner of Hamlet, and was fearful that in his madness he would do her some harm. She cried out for help. Just then, a voice was heard from behind the hangings, 'Help, help the Queen!'

When Hamlet heard this, he was sure that it was the King himself there concealed! At once, he drew out his sword and stabbed at the place where the voice came from! He kept on stabbing until the voice ceased. When he was contented that the King was dead, he dragged forth the body. But to his utter surprise it was not the King, but Polonius, the old, officious counsellor, who had planted himself as a spy behind the hangings.

'Oh, me!' exclaimed the Queen, 'what a rash and bloody deed have you done!'

'A bloody deed, mother,' replied Hamlet, 'but not so bad as yours, who killed a King, and married his brother.'

Glossary
Contented satisfied

Hamlet had gone too far with his words to leave off here. He was now in the mood to speak plainly to his mother, and he did. And though the faults of parents are to be tenderly treated by their children, yet in the case of great crimes the son

may have to speak even to his own mother with some harshness. This harshness is meant for her good and to turn her away from her wicked ways. And now this virtuous prince did tell the Queen about the baseness of her offense in forgetting the dead King, his father within such a short time and marrying his brother, a reputed murderer.

'Mother, your act of treachery has made the heavens bow down in shame!'

He showed her two pictures, one of the late King, her first husband, and the other of the present King, her second husband, and he showed her the difference.

'This man,' he said, 'HAD BEEN your husband.' And then, he showed her whom she had got in his place.

The Queen was extremely ashamed at this. Hamlet asked her how she could continue to live with this man, and be a wife to him, who had murdered her first husband and got the crown by false means. And just as he spoke the ghost of his father, such as he was in his lifetime, entered the room. 'Father, what is the matter? What do you want?' asked Hamlet, terrified.

Glossary
Virtuous possessing high moral standards
Treachery betraying trust or faith

'I came to remind you that you have promised me to take revenge!' said the ghost of the King.

It then vanished, and was seen by none but Hamlet. No description could make his mother perceive it, who was terribly frightened to hear him talking to nothing! She thought that it was all due to his mental disorder. Hamlet begged her not to think that it was his madness, and not her own offenses, which had brought his father's spirit again on the Earth. He also begged of her, with tears, to confess her guilt, and for the future to avoid the company of the King and be no more his wife. Hamlet's pleadings had moved his mother and she promised to abide by his directions. And so, the conference ended. After the conference when Hamlet was at leisure, he was extremely sad to see that it was Polonius who was killed, the father of the lady Ophelia whom he so dearly loved! He wept sadly for what he had done.

The unfortunate death of Polonius gave the King a cause for sending Hamlet out of the kingdom. He would willingly put him to death fearing him to be dangerous; but he dreaded the people, who loved

Hamlet, and the Queen, who, doted upon the prince, her son. So this wicked King, under the pretext of Hamlet's safety that he might not be answerable for Polonius's death, send him off to England, under the care of two courtiers. He despatched letters to the English court, that Hamlet should be put to death as soon as he landed on the English soil.

Hamlet, suspecting some treachery, at night secretly got hold of the letters, and, skillfully erasing his own name, he put in the names of those two courtiers, who had the charge of him, to be put to death. Then he sealed up the letters and put them into their place again. Soon after, the ship was attacked by pirates, and a sea-fight began. In the course of this fight Hamlet, desirous to show his courage boarded the enemy's vessel alone; while his own ship, left him to his fate. The two courtiers made their way to England, carrying those letters the sense of which Hamlet had altered. Immediately on reaching, they met their death.

The pirates who had the prince in their power behaved very gently with Hamlet in the hope that the prince might recompense for any favour they might show him. With this hope, they set Hamlet on the shore at

Glossary
Despatched to send something to a particular place for a purpose
Recompense to repay or to compensate

the nearest port in Denmark. From that place Hamlet wrote to the King, telling him about the strange chance which had brought him back to his own country. He also told the King that on the next day he would present himself before his Majesty.

When Hamlet reached home that day he became a part of a sad happening. It was the funeral of the young and beautiful Ophelia, the lady whom he loved dearly. The mental stability of this young lady had begun to go down ever since her poor father's death. She was shocked and hurt at the fact that her father should die such a painful death that too in the hands of the man whom she loved! She was so affected that in a little time grew completely insane. She would go about giving flowers away to the ladies of the court, saying that they were for her father's burial, singing songs about love and about death, some of which sometimes had no meaning at all.

There was a willow which grew slanting over a brook, and its leaves stooped on the stream. To this brook she came one day with garlands she had been making with daisies and nettles and tried to hang her garland upon the branch of the willow. Not being able to withstand

Glossary
Insane mentally ill

her weight, the branch broke and threw this fair young maid, into the water. Within a short while, her garments became heavy as they became wet resulting in a muddy and miserable death. When Hamlet arrived Laertes, Ophelia's brother was celebrating her funeral. The King and the Queen along with the entire court were present there.

Hamlet being totally unaware of whose buriel ceremony was going on stood on one side, not wishing to interrupt the ceremony. He saw the flowers strewn upon her grave, as the custom was in maiden burials. The Queen herself threw in and said, 'I thought I would make you my Hamlet's wife, had not death taken you away from us!'

Hamlet also saw Laertes leap into the grave and say, 'Cover me also with earth as I wish to be with my dear Ophelia in the grave!'

When Hamlet heard this he realized what was happening! His love for this fair maid came back to him. He could not bear that a brother should show so much grief, for he thought that he loved Ophelia better than forty thousand brothers! And so, he leaped into the grave where Laertes was. Laertes, knowing him to be Hamlet, who had been the cause of his father's and his sister's death, caught him by the throat as an enemy, till the attendants parted them. And Hamlet, after the funeral, excused his hasty act in

throwing himself into the grave.

But Hamlet's wicked uncle, saw an excellent opportunity in this to destroy Hamlet. He convinced Laertes, under cover of peace and reconciliation, to challenge Hamlet to a friendly game of fencing, which Hamlet accepted. A day was appointed to hold the match. At this match all the court was present, and Laertes, by direction of the King, prepared a poisoned weapon. On this match, great wagers were laid by the courtiers, as both Hamlet and Laertes were known to excel at this sword play. Hamlet, taking up the fencing sword, chose one, not at all suspecting the treachery of Laertes. And so, he did even examine Laertes's weapon, who, instead of a fencing sword or blunted sword, made use of a sword which had a sharp and poisoned point.

At first, Laertes did but play with Hamlet, and let him to gain some advantages. At this, the clever King praised Hamlet and drunk to his success. But after a few pauses Laertes, made a deadly thrust at Hamlet with his poisoned weapon and gave him a deadly blow. Hamlet was enraged, but not knowing the whole treachery, in the scuffle exchanged his own innocent

Glossary
Reconcilition the act of reconciling
Excel be exceptionally good at some activity
Advantage a favourable or beneficial event

weapon for Laertes's deadly one. And with a thrust of Laertes's own sword repaid Laertes, with a deady blow which caused his death.

When all the spectators were completely engrossed with the fencing match, suddenly the Queen shrieked out that she was poisoned! She had inadvertently drunk out of a bowl which the king had prepared for Hamlet thinking that if Hamlet survived the fencing match, then he would call him for a drink. The wicked King had forgotten to warn the Queen of the bowl, which she drank from and immediately died.

Hamlet, suspecting some treachery, ordered the doors to be shut while he tried to find out the traitor. But he was interrupted by Laertes who told him to seek no farther, for he was the traitor! And realizing that he was dying due to the wound which Hamlet had given him, Laertes made his confession of his treachery. 'Dear Hamlet, forgive me if you can for my treachery. I have wounded you with my poisoned sword. You have not more than half an hour to live. But trust me, I have not contrived all this. All this was planned by the King himself who wants you dead!' Saying this, Laertes died.

Glossary
Shrieked to make a loud, piercing cry
Traitor a person who betrays someone

When Hamlet saw that his end was drawing near, and there was some poison left upon the sword, he suddenly turned upon his false uncle and thrust the point of the sword into his heart, fulfilling the promise which he had made to his father's spirit! Then Hamlet, feeling his breath fail and his life leaving him, turned to his dear friend Horatio and said, 'Horatio, my dear friend, you must not kill yourself with me but live to tell my story to the world after I die.'

And Horatio promised that he would make a true report as one who was witness to all the circumstances. And, thus satisfied, Hamlet breathed his last and Horatio and the bystanders shed many tears. They remembered how this sweet prince was the beloved of all and how he would have proved to be a competent King of Denmark had he lived.

Glossary
Thrust to push suddenly and violently in a particular direction
Bystanders people who are present at an event or incident but do not take part in it

Post-reading Activities

Let's see if you remember

1. Who was Hamlet? Write a brief character sketch of him.

2. Name the people who informed Hamlet about the appearance of the ghost of his father.

3. What did the ghost of his father tell Hamlet about his murder?

4. What did Hamlet do to verify whether Claudius his uncle was the real murderer of his father?

5. What hurt Hamlet more—his father's death or his mother's marriage to his uncle?

6. What was Hamlet's reaction towards his mother's infidelity?

7. Name the lady whom Hamlet loved. Why and how did she die?

8. Who was Polonius and how did he die?

9. What is the role of Laertes?

10. Critics often say that 'death' forms an important theme in this play. Do you agree with this. Give reasons for your answer.

11. Suggest an alternative title of the play.

12. How did Hamlet's mother die?

About the Author

William Shakespeare was an English poet and playwright, universally acknowledged to be the greatest writer in English language. He is considered to be the world's pre-eminent dramatist also. He lived in the age of Queen Elizabeth I when England enjoyed a time of immense prosperity and stability. He is often called England's national poet and the 'Bard of Avon'.

It is indeed strange that though Shakespeare is recognized as one of literature's greatest influences, very little is actually known about him. Whatever we know about his life comes from the registrar records,

Glossary

Playwright a person who composes plays

court records, wills, marriage certificates and his tombstone.

Early Life

William Shakespeare was born in Stratford-on-Avon, the son of John Shakespeare, a glove maker and dealer in wool. John was a prominent man in Stratford. William's mother was Mary Arden who was the youngest daughter in her family. She inherited much of her father's landowning and farming estate when he died. William was the third child of John and Mary Shakespeare.

Shakespeare probably attended Stratford Grammar School in his childhood. When he was 18, he married Anne Hathaway in 1582. At that time Anne was 26, and already three months pregnant. After sometime his daughter, Susanna, was born. It is generally thought that he must have been in Stratford when Hamnet and Judith, his other two children were born in 1585.

Between the years 1580s and 1592, what Shakespeare did is unknown because no records of his life and works exist of that period. This period of time is often referred to as the 'lost years'. It is possible that he spent this entire period in London after leaving Stratford to escape a charge of deer poaching. Some records say that he was employed at a playhouse 'in a very mean Rank' during this time. Researchers make assumptions that during these 'lost years', Shakespeare might have tended horses for theatergoers or worked as a sailor, a teacher or a coachman. Some think that he might have been a soldier, a law clerk, a theater page, or a moneylender. He could have held several of these jobs or he may have held none of them!

Shakespeare may also have spent the time travelling to far off towns or even to foreign countries. His plays suggest that he visited Italy, for more than a dozen of them including *The Merchant of Venice, Romeo and Juliet, All's Well That Ends Well, Othello, Coriolanus, Julius Caesar, The Two Gentlemen of Verona, The Taming of the Shrew, Titus Andronicus, Much Ado About Nothing*, and *The Winter's Tale*, all have scenes set in Italy.

Career

How Shakespeare first started his career in the theatre no one knows for certain. Whether an acting troupe recruited Shakespeare in his hometown or he was forced on his own to travel to London to begin his career, is not clearly known. In the year 1592 came the first reference to Shakespeare in the world of theatre when Robert Greene an eminent writer of that time mentioned him in his writing. While in London, Shakespeare lived alone in rented accommodations while his wife and children remained in Stratford. Why his family did not move to London with him is unknown.

In 1592, when an epidemic of plague closed the theatres, the versatile Shakespeare wrote sonnets and other poetry until the theatres reopened in 1594. The same year, he joined a newly formed drama group called the 'Lord Chamberlain's Men', serving there as a writer and an actor.

Shakespeare produced most of his well-known works between 1589 and 1613. His early plays were mainly comedies and histories, the literary genre which he raised to the peak of artistic sophistication by the end of the 16th century. He then wrote mainly tragedies until about 1608, including *Hamlet*, *King Lear*, *Othello*, and *Macbeth*, all of which are considered to be the finest works in the English language. In the last

Glossary
Versatile able to adapt to many different functions or activities

years of his career, he wrote tragicomedies, also known as romances, and collaborated with other playwrights.

Shakespeare's works are the greatest representation of art from Elizabethan England. They encompass the economic, social, and educational aspects of life in a nice, neat package. No other art form, including painting, could provide so much information about life in Elizabethan England.

Theatre in Shakespeare's Times

During the age of Shakespeare, all plays which were written had to be approved by the government's censor. This is because plays at that time were considered morally or politically offensive and could be banned. It was considered so very offensive that many a time the playwright would be imprisoned too.

Shakespeare presented his plays at inns, courtyards, royal palaces, private residences, playhouses and the Globe Theatre built in 1599. The playhouses in Shakespeare's time were wooden structures with tiers of seating galleries in the shape of a horseshoe. They could seat two thousand to three thousand people who paid two or more pennies. It is believed that at that

Glossary
Imprisoned kept in prison in a captive state

time the theatre lovers who were wealthy could pay extra to sit on the stage! The main floor, which was surrounded by the galleries, had no roof and no seats. A person could stand and watch the play standing by paying a penny. This area was called a 'pit'. Up to one thousand people could stand and watch performances in this area under a hot sun or dark clouds.

The stage of the Globe theatre was four to six feet above ground level. There was no curtain that opened or closed at the beginning or at the end of the plays. A wall with two or three doors leading to the dressing rooms of the actors stood at the back of the stage. These rooms collectively were known as the 'tiring house'.

Males played all the characters, even that of women! Actors played gods, ghosts, demons, and other supernatural characters. They could pop up from the underworld through a trap door on the stage or descend down to Earth from heaven on a winch line from the ceiling. The sound of thunder was created off stage, by beating a sheet metal. To demonstrate that an actor had suffered a fencing wound, he simply had to slap his hand against a pouch beneath his shirt to release 'blood' showing his death.

Globe Theatre

Although Shakespeare's plays were performed at different venues during the playwright's career, the Globe Theatre in the Southwark district of London was the place at which his best known plays were first performed. The Globe was built during Shakespeare's early period in 1599 by one of his long-standing associates, Cuthbert Burbage.

The theater that Cuthbert Burbage built had a total capacity between 2,000 and 3,000 spectators. Due to the absence of electric lights, all performances at the Globe were conducted during the day (probably in the mid-afternoon spanning between 2 p.m. and 5 p.m.). As most of the stage of the Globe Theatre was open air and the apparatus for sound system were poor, the actors were compelled to shout their lines, stress their intonations, and engage themselves in exaggerated theatrical gestures. The plays which were staged at the Globe were completely devoid of background scenery although costumes and props were utilized. There was no proscenium arch, no curtains, and no stagehands than the actors themselves. Instead, changes of scenes

Glossary
Spectator a person who watches something—a show, a game, or any other event
Apparatus the equipment or machinery needed for a particular activity

were suggested in the speeches and narrative situations of the plays.

End of Globe Theatre

The original structure of the Globe Theatre existed until June 29, 1613, when its thatched roof was set on fire by a cannon fired during the performance of the play Henry VIII. The Globe burned to ashes and could not be saved. At this time, Shakespeare had almost retired and was at Stratford-on-Avon where he died three years later at the age of fifty-two. The Globe was reconstructed in the year 1614.

Glossary
Proscenium arch it is a kind of an arch which forms a framing on the opening between the stage and the auditorium in some theatres